READY TO REPORT

written by Ellen Sussman
illustrated by Priscilla Burris

ELLEN SUSSMAN graduated from Brooklyn College and has taught with the New York City Board of Education, the School District of Philadelphia and the Los Angeles Unified School District as a classroom teacher and reading specialist.

PRISCILLA BURRIS received an Associate of Arts degree in Creative Design from the Fashion Institute of Design and Merchandising in Los Angeles. As a free-lance artist of child-related artwork, she has been drawing since she was one year old.

Reproduction of these pages by the classroom teacher for use in the classroom and not for commercial use is permissible. Reproduction of these pages for an entire school or school district is strictly prohibited.

Copyright 1988 by **THE MONKEY SISTERS, INC.**
22971 Via Cruz
Laguna Niguel, CA 92677

ISBN 0-933606-66-4

Report Card

Topic: _____

Student's Name _____ Date_____

Grading System:
        1-2 = Unsatisfactory
        3-4 = Poor
        5-6 = Fair/Average
        7-8 = Good
        9-10 = Excellent

1. Used sufficient sources: _____
2. Selected important information for notes: _____
3. Used good paragraph development from notes: _____
4. Used complete sentences with correct spelling, punctuation and grammar: _____
5. Wrote neatly and legibly: _____
6. Included all necessary information and presented it in sequential order: _____
7. Writing was done in an interesting manner that was pleasant to read: _____
8. Showed creativity in title and cover design: _____
9. Showed evidence of being organized and following directions: _____
10. Submitted work on time: _____

     Submitted work for extra credit: _____

Comments:

TOTAL SCORE: _____ (top score = 100 points + extra credit)

To The Teacher

READY TO REPORT introduces the skills of beginning research, note-taking and report writing in a format of guided steps. Students will be required to research each topic using encyclopedias, almanacs and library books, as well as magazines, picture files, photographs and other references you may assign.

Each unit presents a student planning sheet and note-taking pages. A report card is included where you can evaluate each student's work on different levels for each report.

Prior to assigning the first unit, children should be familiar with the encyclopedia and its location in the media center, school library and local library. You may wish to have the school or local librarian give a beginning lesson on reference materials and note-taking.

It is suggested that the first unit be done as a class project. Assign one of the reports where the whole class has the same topic—whales, Alaska, Prince Charles, etc.—so that each student can be working on the same part of the assignment simultaneously. The teacher or aide should check each page of notes prior to the student going on to the next page. You may want to assign specific times for small groups to use reference materials at this stage.

To get students to develop interesting paragraphs from their notes, include a few lessons using other topics. List 8-10 notes on the chalkboard and have students use these notes to write an interesting paragraph. Suggested topics for this introductory paragraph lessons are: animals, television shows, a current events story.

Once all the "note-taking" pages have been completed and students are familiar with writing interesting paragraphs from their notes, they may work independently to write their report. Students should submit their note-taking pages along with their written report.

At this last stage, let students know of any additional requirements . . . . you may wish to permit students to hand in computer-printed or typewritten reports vs. handwritten copy only.

Allow about three weeks for each report unit initially. Two-week time frames may be suitable once students are more adept at report writing.

Table of Contents

Whales	Pages 1-9
Alaska	Pages 10-18
The Statue of Liberty	Pages 19-27
Prince Charles	Pages 28-34
The Olympics	Pages 35-43
Biography	Pages 44-52
Foreign Lands	Pages 53-61
Famous Landmarks	Pages 62-68
Answer Key	Pages 69-71

Name _____

Student Planning Sheet for Report on Whales

Your assignment is to do research on whales and use the facts to write a report.

You may use some or all of the following resource materials in gathering your information:
- encyclopedias
- library books
- booklets and pamphlets obtained from aquariums
- magazines
- filmstrips, videos or television shows about whales
- illustrations and photographs

For the first part of this assignment, you will *write notes* in the frames on the following pages. This information does not need to be in complete sentences. Write only enough words to use later in writing your report.

The following guide will help you in organizing your work:
- Use *at least three* sources to gather your facts. Keep a bibliography of all your sources—title, author, publisher, copyright date, issue, volume, etc.
- Look at pictures and photographs to learn about the different kinds of whales.
- Fill in the following pages with facts as you do your research.
- When these pages are complete, you will be ready to use the notes to write your report.
- Do not throw away your note pages. You will need to submit them along with your written report.

Writing your report:
- Use the facts on the *Introductory Information* page to develop your opening paragraph.
- Plan the rest of your report—writing one paragraph for each page of notes—in the following order:
  - —whale words
  - —appearance
  - —size
  - —baleen whales
  - —toothed whales
  - —feeding and migration
- Your last paragraph should be a conclusion and interesting summary.
- If you wish to earn "Extra Credit" complete the activities and submit this work with your report.
- List your sources on a separate sheet titled 'Bibliography.' This page will follow your page on feeding and migration.
- Reread your report. Make any changes and correct any errors.
- Rewrite your report using a neat, legible handwriting.
- The report should be complete and ready to submit by _____
- Design an appealing cover and give your report an interesting title.

Ready to Report © THE MONKEY SISTERS, INC.

Introductory Information

What is a whale? Describe its unique features.

Name two groups of whales. What is the main difference between the two groups?

Are whales mammals or fish? List three facts to support your answer.
Whales are _____ because:

1.

2.

3.

Which group do dolphins and porpoises belong to? Why?

Ready to Report © THE MONKEY SISTERS, INC.

Whale Words

Write the definition of each word:

Blubber:

Blowhole:

Fluke:

Baleen:

Ambergris:

Appearance

What does a whale look like? Describe the appearance of each feature below.

- head

- flippers

- tail

- skin

What other features do you consider special to whales?

Ready to Report © THE MONKEY SISTERS, INC.

Size

What is the largest whale? How large is it?

How long are whales? Describe the range from shortest to longest?

How much do whales weigh? Describe the range from lightest to heaviest?

How many years does it take a whale to reach its adult size?

Are dolphins and porpoises considered large or small whales?
How long is a dolphin? _____
How long is a porpoise? _____

Ready to Report © THE MONKEY SISTERS, INC.

Baleen Whales

Describe the unusual feature of baleen whales.

How many blowholes do they have?

List the three groups of baleen whales. For each group, note one feature that is special. This feature may be about size, color, appearance, what they eat, the waters they swim in, etc.

Ready to Report © THE MONKEY SISTERS, INC.

 # Toothed Whales

How are toothed whales different from baleen whales?

List the five groups of toothed whales. For each group, note one feature that is special. This feature may be about size, color, appearance, what they eat, the waters they swim in, etc.

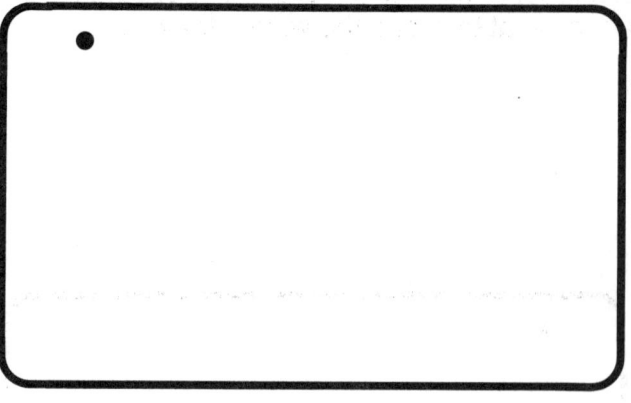

Ready to Report © THE MONKEY SISTERS, INC.

Feeding and Migration

What do baleen whales feed on?

What do sperm whales feed on?

Describe the migration of the California gray whales and humpback whales when they leave the waters of the Arctic and Antarctic oceans. Where do they migrate to? When do they return?

 # Extra Credit

Use a non-fiction library book about whales and list three facts about whales that interested you. These should be facts *not written in your notes as an answer to a previous question.*

Some suggested books are:
1. *Whales: Their Life in the Sea* by Faith McNulty
2. *Whales* by Valerie Pitt
3. *Whales and Dolphins* by Francene Sabin
4. *The Whale Watcher's Guide* by Robert Gardner
5. *The Way of the Dolphin* by Dr. Michael Fox

List the title and author of the book you got your facts from in your bibliography.

Choose one of the following art/craft projects to submit with your written report.

1. Make a papier-mache model of one kind of whale. Attach a tag that tells what kind of whale it is.

2. Create a 3-dimensional map that shows the waters where whales live and the waters they migrate to. Show the continents and label your map.

3. Create a scrapbook showing at least six different whales. Include pictures, drawings or photographs. Describe each whale under the illustration.

4. Use a variety of fabrics, papers or other materials of your choice and create a 3-dimensional whale. Attach it to a backing board. Label it to describe what materials you used.

Ready to Report © THE MONKEY SISTERS, INC.

Name _____

Student Planning Sheet for Report on Alaska

Your assignment is to do research on the state of Alaska and use the facts to write a report.

You may use some or all of the following resource materials in gathering your information:
- encyclopedias
- almanacs
- atlases
- library books
- brochures from travel agents, airlines and cruise ship companies
- magazines
- filmstrips, videos or television shows about Alaska

For the first part of this assignment, you will *write notes* in the frames on the following pages. This information does not need to be in complete sentences. Write only enough words to use later in writing your report.

The following guide will help you in organizing your work:
- Use *at least three* sources to gather your facts. Keep a bibliography of all your sources—title, author, publisher, copyright date, issue, volume, etc.
- Look at pictures and photographs to learn about the different people and the land in Alaska.
- Fill in the following pages with facts as you do your research.
- When these pages are complete, you will be ready to use the notes to write your report.
- Do not throw away your note pages. You will need to submit them along with your written report.

Writing your report:
- Use the facts on the *Introductory Information* page to develop your opening paragraph.
- Plan the rest of your report—writing one paragraph for each page of notes—in the following order:
  —geography
  —climate
  —animal life
  —industry
  —agriculture
  —Eskimos
- Your last paragraph should be a conclusion and interesting summary.
- The map of Alaska showing its boundaries will follow the written report.
- List your sources on a separate sheet titled 'Bibliography.' This page will follow your map.
- Reread your report. Make any changes and correct any errors.
- Rewrite your report using a neat, legible handwriting.
- The report should be complete and ready to submit by _____
- Design an appealing cover and give your report an interesting title.

Introductory Information

What does the word *Alaska* mean?

How large is Alaska in square miles? Describe its size in comparison to the continental United States or Canada.

What is the state capital?

What is the largest city?

What is the highest point? Where is it?

Describe and draw the state flag.

Ready to Report © THE MONKEY SISTERS, INC.

Geography

What are the names of the four major land regions in Alaska?

What are the two principal rivers in Alaska?

What region has Alaska's most productive farmland?

In what part of Alaska is the Alaska Peninsula and Aleutian Islands found? How many large and small islands make up the Aleutian Islands?

Ready to Report © THE MONKEY SISTERS, INC.

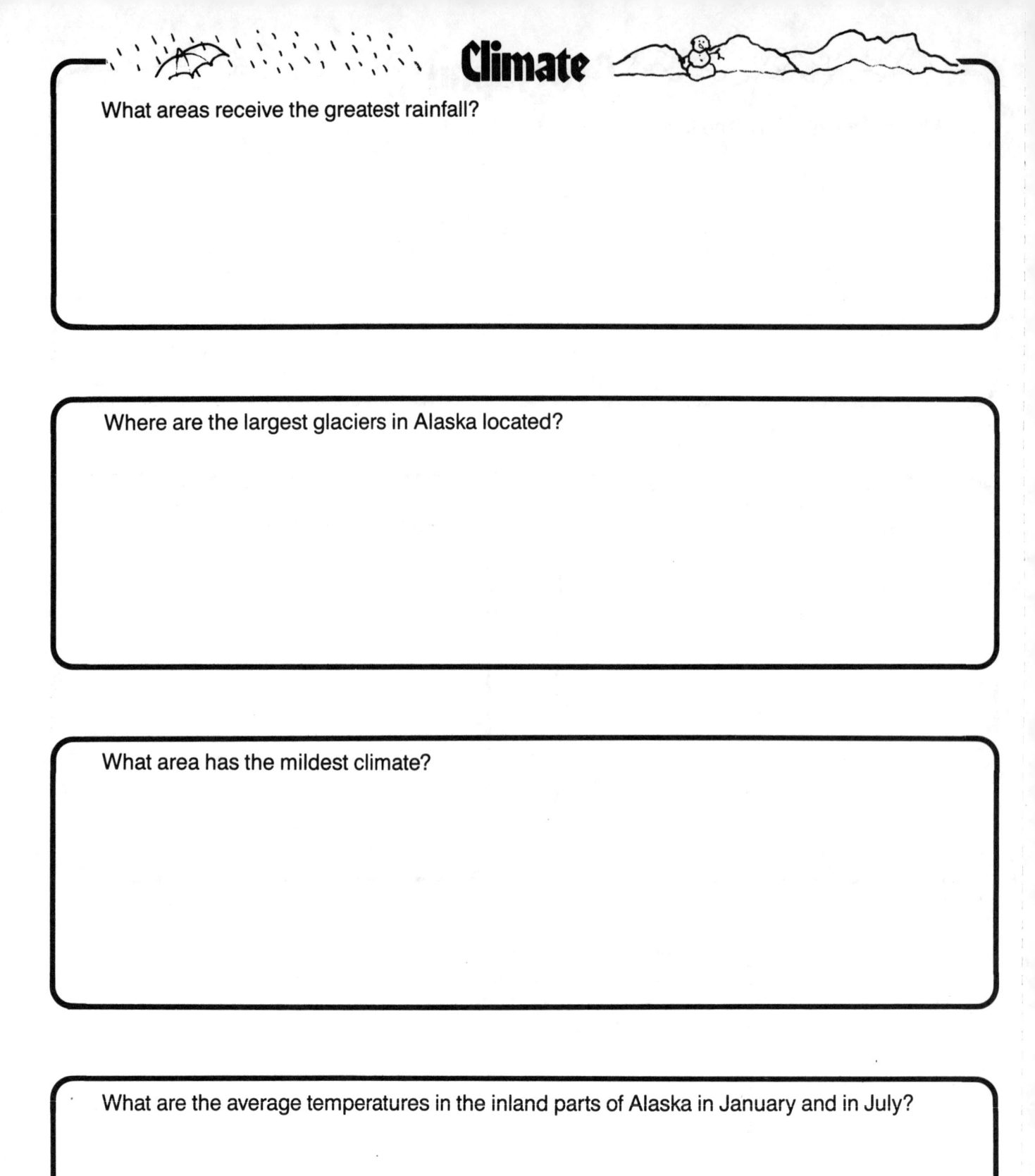

Climate

What areas receive the greatest rainfall?

Where are the largest glaciers in Alaska located?

What area has the mildest climate?

What are the average temperatures in the inland parts of Alaska in January and in July?

Animal Life

Alaska's rich and varied animal life has been of important economic value. Describe the animal life in each group below. How has each group been important to industry and to the economy of Alaska?

- fish

- sea mammals

- big game animals

- fur-bearing animals

Ready to Report © THE MONKEY SISTERS, INC.

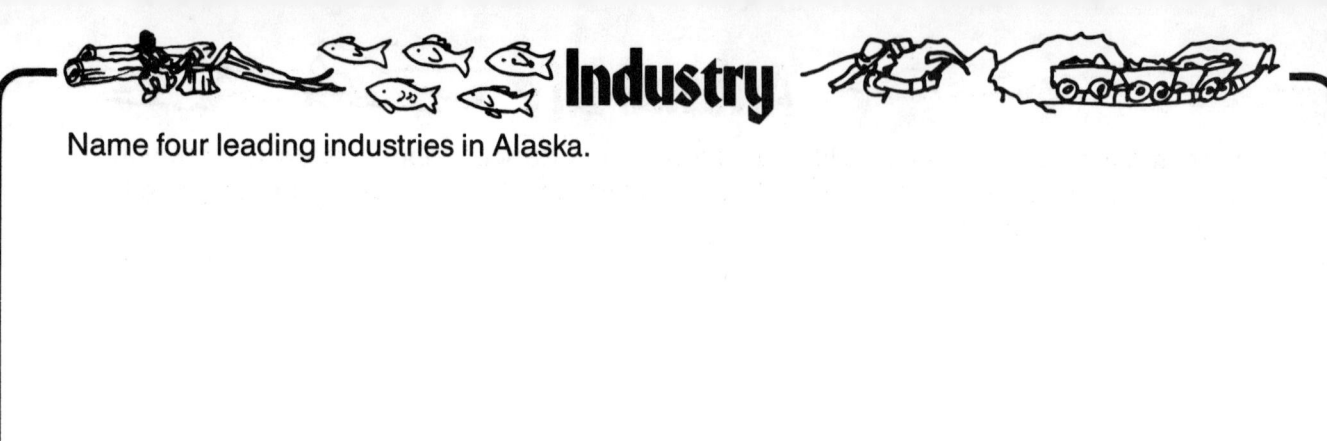

Industry

Name four leading industries in Alaska.

What fuels have been found in abundance in Alaska?

What are three main sources of work in Alaska?

15   Ready to Report © THE MONKEY SISTERS, INC.

Agriculture

Alaska's long hours of summer sunlight are an aid to growing many crops. Which crops grow well and are farmed in Alaska?

In what parts of Alaska is the dairy industry most productive?

What berries grow well in Alaska?

What kinds of grain grow well in the interior region?

What are the main livestock products?

Ready to Report © THE MONKEY SISTERS, INC.

 # Eskimos

Although Eskimos are only one of the native races in Alaska, they are an interesting people to learn about. Describe the physical features of Eskimos. What do they look like?

What parts of Alaska do Eskimos mainly live in?

Eskimos are known to work well with their hands. What are two crafts they do well?

In what jobs and industries are Eskimos employed?

17

Ready to Report © THE MONKEY SISTERS, INC.

Boundaries and Map

What are the boundaries of Alaska? Draw a map and label the boundaries.

Name _____

STUDENT PLANNING SHEET FOR REPORT ON THE STATUE OF LIBERTY

Your assignment is to do research on the Statue of Liberty and use the facts to write a report.

You may use some or all of the following resource materials in gathering your information:
- encyclopedias
- almanacs
- library books
- filmstrips or videos about this subject
- magazines
- tourist guides

For the first part of this assignment, you will *write notes* in the frames on the following pages. This information does not need to be in complete sentences. Write only enough words to use later in writing your report.

The following guide will help you in organizing your work:
- Use *at least three* sources to gather your facts. Keep a bibliography of all your sources—title, author, publisher, copyright date, issue, volume, etc.
- Look at pictures and photographs to learn about the Statue of Liberty.
- Fill in the following pages with facts as you do your research.
- When these pages are complete, you will be ready to use the notes to write your report.
- Do not throw away your note pages. You will need to submit them along with your written report.

Writing your report:
- Use the facts on the *Introductory Information* page to develop your opening paragraph.
- Plan the rest of your report—writing one paragraph for each page of notes—in the following order:
  - —building the statue
  - —sculptors and builders
  - —symbols of liberty
  - —the inscription
  - —restoration
  - —the island today
- Your last paragraph should be a conclusion and interesting summary.
- The "Facts and Figures" page will follow the written report.
- List your sources on a separate sheet titled 'Bibliography.' This page will follow your facts and figures page.
- Reread your report. Make any changes and correct any errors.
- Rewrite your report using a neat, legible handwriting.
- The report should be complete and ready to submit by _____
- Design an appealing cover and give your report an interesting title.

Introductory Information

Where is the Statue of Liberty located? Name the island, the body of water and the city that surrounds it.

What was the original name of the island? In what year was the name changed?

When was the statue dedicated?

Describe the sequence of events that enabled immigrants to first see the Statue of Liberty when they came to the United States in the latter part of the 19th and earlier part of the 20th centuries.

Ready to Report © THE MONKEY SISTERS, INC.

Building the Statue

Where was the statue built? How long did it take?

What parts were built first? How did these parts, when finished, help raise money for the rest of the statue?

What country paid for building the statue? How was money raised?

What country paid for building the pedestal? How was money raised?

What problems arose because the statue was being built and paid for by two countries?

SCULPTORS AND BUILDERS

Who was the sculptor who built the Statue of Liberty? What country was he from?

Who constructed the 'skeleton' for the statue? What else is this person famous for?

Who designed the pedestal for the statue?

Describe how the statue was shipped to the United States.

Ready to Report © THE MONKEY SISTERS, INC.

SYMBOLS OF LIBERTY

The Statue of Liberty is a symbol of liberty, freedom and opportunity. Various parts of the statue are especially symbolic.

In her right hand, the statue holds a torch or beacon of light. What does this represent?

In her left hand, the statue holds a tablet inscribed with a date in Roman numerals. What is this date and what does it signify?

The crown has seven spikes. What do they represent?

The statue has a broken chain at her feet. Her left foot is thrust forward. What does this signify?

Ready to Report © THE MONKEY SISTERS, INC.

The Inscription

An American poet wrote a poem called "The New Colossus" in 1883. Who was this poet?

The closing lines of the poem were inscribed on a tablet on the pedestal in 1903. What are these famous lines?

Why do you think these lines were chosen as the inscription?

Ready to Report © THE MONKEY SISTERS, INC.

24

Restoration

In what year did the restoration begin?

Describe the goal of the Statue of Liberty—Ellis Island Centennial Commission. How did they raise money?

What did restoration include? Describe at least five items that were restored.

What celebration occurred when the restoration was completed? What date was the celebration?

The Island Today

Why does the statue's outer skin appear green even after restoration?

Describe the museum located inside the pedestal if you were to visit the statue today.

How is the Statue of Liberty maintained? Tell what organization oversees the care of the statue.

Facts and Figures

The Statue of Liberty's Measurements:

Height from foundation to torch: _____

Height from base to torch: _____

Height of torch: _____

Distance across an eye: _____

Length of nose: _____

Width of mouth: _____

Length of right arm: _____

Size of fingernail: _____

Length of tablet: _____

Width of tablet: _____

Total weight: _____

Steps from base to crown: _____

Steps in pedestal: _____

Windows in crown: _____

Spikes in crown: _____

Several names have been used to describe the Statue of Liberty. List at least three of these other than "Statue of Liberty."

Name _____

Student Planning Sheet for Report on Prince Charles

Your assignment is to do research on Prince Charles and use the facts to write a report.

You may use some or all of the following resource materials in gathering your information:
- encyclopedias
- library books
- magazines and newspapers
- filmstrips or videos about Prince Charles
- television shows and news broadcasts about Prince Charles
- history books

For the first part of this assignment, you will *write notes* in the frames on the following pages. This information does not need to be in complete sentences. Write only enough words to use later in writing your report.

The following guide will help you in organizing your work:
- Use *at least three* sources to gather your facts. Keep a bibliography of all your sources—title, author, publisher, copyright date, issue, volume, etc.
- Look at pictures and photographs to learn about Prince Charles, his family and his life in England.
- Fill in the following pages with facts as you do your research.
- When these pages are complete, you will be ready to use the notes to write your report.
- Do not throw away your note pages. You will need to submit them along with your written report.

Writing your report:
- Use the facts on the *Introductory Information* page to develop your opening paragraph.
- Plan the rest of your report—writing one paragraph for each page of notes—in the following order:
  - —the royal family
  - —childhood
  - —early education
  - —later education
  - —adult life
- Your last paragraph should be a conclusion and interesting summary.
- Attach some recent newspaper photographs and photocopy pictures from magazines and include these at the end of your written report.
- List your sources on a separate sheet titled 'Bibliography.' This page will follow your photographs.
- Reread your report. Make any changes and correct any errors.
- Rewrite your report using a neat, legible handwriting.
- The report should be complete and ready to submit by _____
- Design an appealing cover and give your report an interesting title.

Ready to Report © THE MONKEY SISTERS, INC.

Introductory Information

What is a monarchy?

How is Prince Charles next in line for the monarchy?

Who are the rulers in a monarchy?

Who is the current monarch in England?

What does the title "Prince of Wales" refer to?

The Royal Family

Define the term 'royalty.'

Describe Prince Charles' family. Give their names and titles.

- parents

- sisters and brothers

- wife and children

Who would be next in line to the British throne after Prince Charles? Explain.

Childhood

Although Queen Elizabeth attempted to give her children a "normal upbringing," several factors would set Prince Charles apart from other children. What were some ways Prince Charles' life was different from other children?

How were Prince Charles' first experiences in school different from most children?

What subjects did he find most difficult?

What sports did Prince Charles begin to show an interest in as a child?

Early Education

At what age did Prince Charles change from being taught at the palace to a regular classroom?

What was the first school he attended outside the palace? Describe the kind of children who attended this school.

What problems arose because Prince Charles attended a school outside the palace.

Describe Prince Charles' school schedule at this early stage in his education.

Ready to Report © THE MONKEY SISTERS, INC.

Later Education

What was the next school Prince Charles attended? Why was this school chosen?

How was attending this school a different experience for him? What problems did he encounter?

What school did Prince Charles attend next? Describe the education and goals of this school.

What were Prince Charles' best subjects?

Ready to Report © THE MONKEY SISTERS, INC.

Adult Life

Describe Prince Charles service in the armed forces of England. What did he serve in and what did he excel in?

Describe his wedding. Include information on his bride's name, the age at which he married, and the date of the wedding. (You may include copies of photographs from books on the last page of your report).

What are Prince Charles' main duties in his daily life?

What sports and recreational activities does he enjoy as an adult?

Ready to Report © THE MONKEY SISTERS, INC.

Name _____

Student Planning Sheet for Report on the Olympics

Your assignment is to do research on the Olympics and use the facts to write a report.

You may use some or all of the following resource materials in gathering your information:
- encyclopedias
- almanacs
- library books
- magazines and newspapers
- television shows about the Olympics
- other printed materials about the Olympics

For the first part of this assignment, you will *write notes* in the frames on the following pages. This information does not need to be in complete sentences. Write only enough words to use later in writing your report.

The following guide will help you in organizing your work:
- Use *at least three* sources to gather your facts. Keep a bibliography of all your sources—title, author, publisher, copyright date, issue, volume, etc.
- Look at pictures and photographs to learn about the different sports and the Olympics.
- Fill in the following pages with facts as you do your research.
- When these pages are complete, you will be ready to use the notes to write your report.
- Do not throw away your note pages. You will need to submit them along with your written report.

Writing your report:
- Use the facts on the *Introductory Information* page to develop your opening paragraph.
- Plan the rest of your report—writing one paragraph for each page of notes—in the following order:
  —the modern Olympics
  —opening ceremonies
  —awards
  —champions
  —competing
  —interesting facts
  —the last Olympics
- Your last paragraph should be a conclusion and interesting summary.
- List your sources on a separate sheet titled 'Bibliography.'
- Reread your report. Make any changes and correct any errors.
- Rewrite your report using a neat, legible handwriting.
- The report should be complete and ready to submit by _____
- Design an appealing cover and give your report an interesting title.

Introductory Information

The ancient Olympics were held by the Greeks. In what year was the first sporting event held? What kind of event was it?

Where was it held? Tell the place and the setting.

Modern Olympics have three winners for each event. How many winners did the ancient Greek Olympics have?

What was the prize?

The ancient Olympic Games ended when the Romans conquered Greece. In what year was that? How many years had the Greek Olympics been held before they ended?

Ready to Report © THE MONKEY SISTERS, INC.

The Modern Olympics

Who was the person credited with starting a new series of Olympic Games? What country was he from?

In what year was the first *modern* Olympic Games held? Where were they held?

The International Olympic Committee was formed. What was its function?

A main rule was that Olympic athletes had to be *amateurs.* What does this mean?

What was the plan for future Olympic Games regarding when and where they would be held?

Opening Ceremonies

The modern Olympics, like the ancient ones, have special ceremonies that are impressive to watch.

No matter which country hosts the Olympics, the athletes from one particular country enter the stadium before the athletes of any other country. What country is this? Why is this done?

An official of the host country declares the games *'open'* and the Olympic flag is raised showing five interlocked rings. What colors are these rings and what do they represent?

Weeks before the Olympics, a burning torch is carried by runners from Olympia, Greece to the site of the games. How is the torch carried?

What does the final runner do?

What happens at the end of the opening ceremonies?

Ready to Report © THE MONKEY SISTERS, INC.

Awards

Most events have elimination rounds before the finals. How many medals are given for each final event?

What are the medals?

What happens in the stadium as the winners receive their medals?

Who can win prizes?

Champions

A number of great Olympic champions have won *several* gold medals in their careers. Make a chart and show the following for at least six Olympic champions.

- the country he or she was from
- how many gold medals he or she has won
- the events
- the years the gold medals were won

Competing

How does a person get to be an Olympic athlete?

Why do you think athletes want to compete at an event that offers medals instead of money?

Approximately how many countries participate? How many sports are there in the games?

List at least six 'winter games' sports.

List at least six 'summer games' sports.

41   Ready to Report © THE MONKEY SISTERS, INC.

Interesting Facts

Why are there separate events for men and women?

How many countries must play the sport in order for the sport to be played in the Olympics?

How many countries must enter the Olympic competition for that sport?

Women could not participate in the 1896 Olympics. When did this change?

Another change occurred in 1924. What was this change?

Olympic Games were scheduled but not held in 1940 and 1944. Why were they not held?

The Last Olympics

What year was the last Olympics held? Where?

Choose one winter sport from these Olympics. Briefly describe the skills needed. Name the athlete who won the gold medal.

Choose one summer sport from these Olympics. Briefly describe the skills needed. Name the athlete who won the gold medal.

Were any new world records set? If so, name the sport and tell how the world's record was changed?

Name _____

Student Planning Sheet for Report on a Biography

Your assignment is to do research on a famous person and use the facts to write a report.

You may use some or all of the following resource materials in gathering your information:
- encyclopedias
- Who's Who in America?
- library books
- magazines
- filmstrips, videos, movies or television shows about this person.

For the first part of this assignment, you will *write notes* in the frames on the following pages. This information does not need to be in complete sentences. Write only enough words to use later in writing your report.

The following guide will help you in organizing your work:
- Use *at least three* sources to gather your facts. Keep a bibliography of all your sources—title, author, publisher, copyright date, issue, volume, etc.
- Look at pictures and photographs to learn about the famous person and his or her life.
- Fill in the following pages with facts as you do your research.
- When these pages are complete, you will be ready to use the notes to write your report.
- Do not throw away your note pages. You will need to submit them along with your written report.

Writing your report:
- Use the facts on the *Introductory Information* page to develop your opening paragraph.
- Plan the rest of your report—writing one paragraph for each page of notes—in the following order:
  —childhood
  —adulthood (two paragraphs)
  —honors and awards
  —major accomplishments
  —lasting impressions
- Your last paragraph should be a conclusion and interesting summary.
- The time-line will follow the written report.
- List your sources on a separate sheet titled 'Bibliography.' This page will follow your time-line.
- Reread your report. Make any changes and correct any errors.
- Rewrite your report using a neat, legible handwriting.
- The report should be complete and ready to submit by _____
- Design an appealing cover and give your report an interesting title.

Ready to Report © THE MONKEY SISTERS, INC.

Introductory Information

What person have you selected to report about? Why did you choose this person?

Where and when was this person born?

Why is this person famous or remembered?

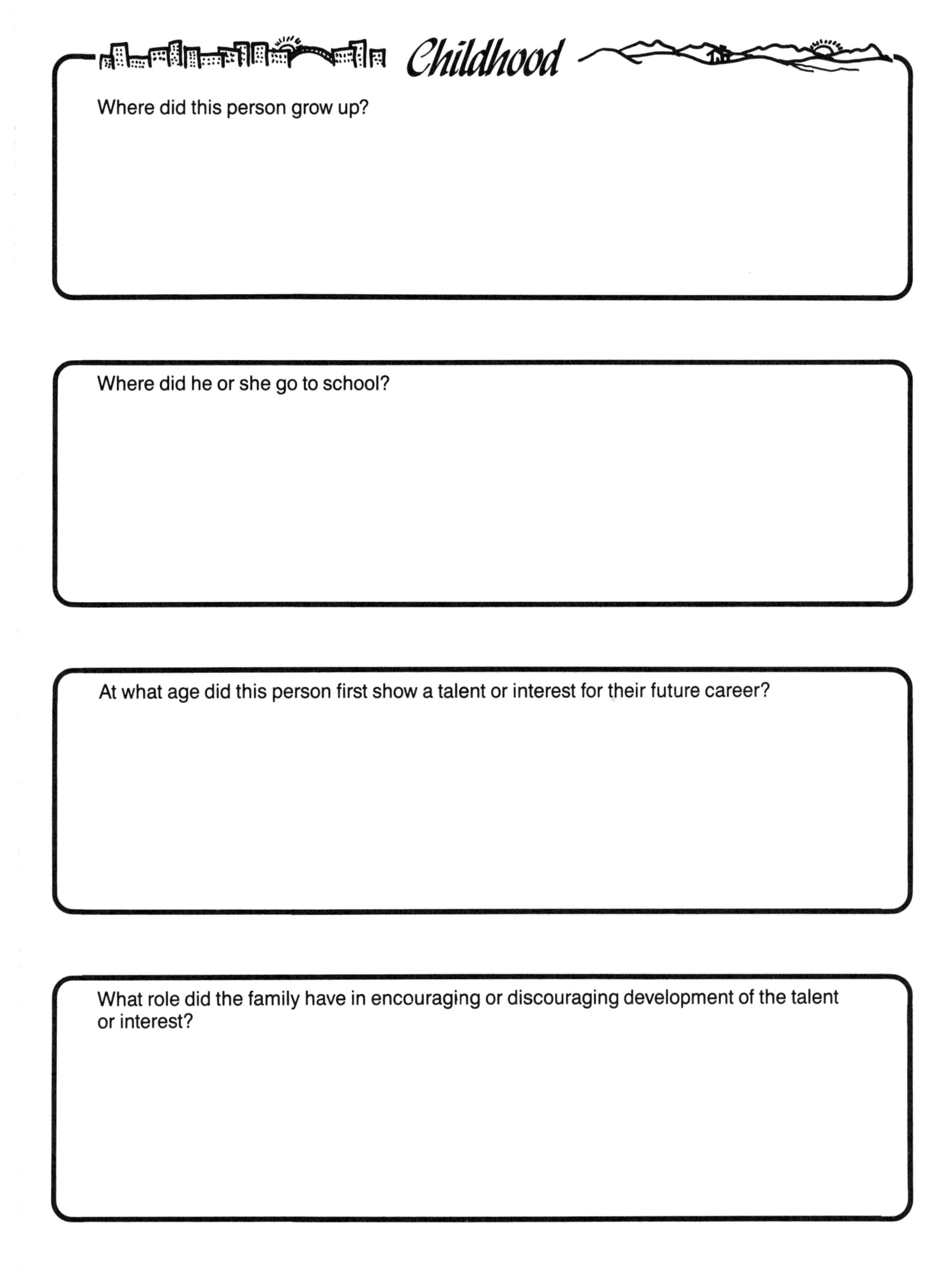

Childhood

Where did this person grow up?

Where did he or she go to school?

At what age did this person first show a talent or interest for their future career?

What role did the family have in encouraging or discouraging development of the talent or interest?

Ready to Report © THE MONKEY SISTERS, INC.

Adulthood

What special training or education did this person have?

At what age did this person first do something that people, other than his or her family, thought was exceptional? What accomplishment was this?

What unusual things happened in this person's life that had an effect on this person's career?

Adulthood

Did this person have any handicaps? Explain.

What special things could this person do?

How was this person's contribution important to his country?

Would you say success was achieved mainly by a natural talent, hard work or luck? Explain.

Honors and Awards

What special honors, awards, medals or prizes did this person receive for his or her work?

What memorials, monuments, buildings, cities, etc., are named in this person's honor? Where is each located?

What was one special event that was a highlight in this person's life once fame was reached? This may be a performance, an exhibit, being invited to meet a world leader, etc.

Major Accomplishments

List ten major accomplishments or works this person is known for. If it is a musician, you may list ten of his most famous works; if it is an inventor, you may list the various steps to success, etc.

1.

2.

3.

4.

5.

6.

7.

8.

9.

10.

Lasting Impressions

How would the world be different if this person had not achieved the accomplishments that made him famous?

When did this person die? How old was he or she?

Why will this person always be remembered?

Tell one way you would like to be the same as this person.

Ready to Report © THE MONKEY SISTERS, INC.

Time-Line

Create a time-line to show the important events in this person's life. Begin with the year of birth and show the year of death as the end. You may divide your time-line into segments of 5-year periods; 10-year periods, etc. that is most suitable for your subject. Show the year of the important event and name the event. (If your subject is still living, indicate this by showing the latest achievements.)

Ready to Report © THE MONKEY SISTERS, INC.

Name _____

Student Planning Sheet for Report on a Foreign Country

Your assignment is to do research on another country and use the facts to write a report.

You may use some or all of the following resource materials in gathering your information:
- encyclopedias
- almanacs
- atlases
- library books
- brochures from travel agents, airlines and cruise ship companies
- magazines
- filmstrips, videos or television shows about this country
- interviewing a person from this country

For the first part of this assignment, you will *write notes* in the frames on the following pages. This information does not need to be in complete sentences. Write only enough words to use later in writing your report.

The following guide will help you in organizing your work:
- Use *at least three* sources to gather your facts. Keep a bibliography of all your sources—title, author, publisher, copyright date, issue, volume, etc.
- Look at pictures and photographs to learn about the people and the country.
- Fill in the following pages with facts as you do your research.
- When these pages are complete, you will be ready to use the notes to write your report.
- Do not throw away your note pages. You will need to submit them along with your written report.

Writing your report:
- Use the facts on the *Introductory Information* page to develop your opening paragraph.
- Plan the rest of your report—writing one paragraph for each page of notes—in the following order:
  - —government
  - —geography
  - —customs
  - —food
  - —famous people
  - —sports and recreation
- Your last paragraph should be a conclusion and interesting summary.
- The map of this country will follow the written report.
- List your sources on a separate sheet titled 'Bibliography.' This page will follow your map.
- Reread your report. Make any changes and correct any errors.
- Rewrite your report using a neat, legible handwriting.
- The report should be complete and ready to submit by _____
- Design an appealing cover and give your report an interesting title.

Ready to Report © THE MONKEY SISTERS, INC.

Introductory Information

What country will your report be about?

What continent is this country on?

What is the principal language spoken in this country?

This country is about _____ square miles. It is close in size to _____.
(a state, province or another country)

Describe the money system in this country. What are names of the different coins? What is the main unit of currency used for spending? (In the United States and Canada, it is the dollar.)

List the most famous landmarks and most popular tourist attractions. In what city is each located?

Government

Briefly describe the government of this country. Tell what form of government rules the country. What is the name of the governing body?

Who is the current leader of the country? What is his or her title?

What is the name of the official government building where laws are made? In what city is it located?

Find a recent newspaper article about this country. Summarize the article. Attach the article to the back of this sheet.

55   Ready to Report © THE MONKEY SISTERS, INC.

Geography

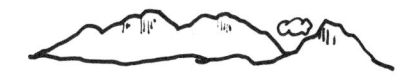

Name the major cities and/or regions where manufacturing is done. Is the city located by a seaport or waterway? Name the product manufactured with each city.

What are the major mountain ranges?

What are the principal waterways? (oceans, rivers, lakes, canals, etc.)

Describe the climate of this country.

List the major products manufactured or grown for export. What countries are the products exported to?

Customs

Describe 2-3 customs of this country that appear unusual to your way of doing it.

Describe 2-3 customs that people in this country would probably find different or unusual that *you* do and consider to be 'ordinary.' (weddings, birthdays, eating habits, etc.)

How would you prepare for a visit to this country?

Describe 2-3 holidays that are celebrated in this country that are not celebrated in yours.

Ready to Report © THE MONKEY SISTERS, INC.

Food

Research to find out how you would say the names of the following foods in the language of the country. Write the word and practice pronouncing it to share with the class.

1. bread _____
2. milk _____
3. meat _____
4. cheese _____
5. apple _____

6. ice cream _____
7. water _____
8. potato _____
9. egg _____
10. fish _____

Name some foods you enjoy eating that originated from this country.

What foods does this country grow, farm or manufacture for export?

What eating customs do the people in this country follow that are different from yours?

Ready to Report ©THE MONKEY SISTERS, INC.

Famous People

Choose three categories from the following: authors and poets, artists and sculptors, musicians and composers, explorers, inventors, world leaders. List the categories and name three people for each one. Describe what each person is best known for.

Name one of the famous persons in your selection. Describe his or her childhood and how it influenced his or her fame.

How would the world be different today if this person did not accomplish what he or she is so well-known for?

Name museums, historical sights, landmarks or memorials in this country that honor this person by showing his or her works or have been built as a monument to their memory. Name the city in which each is located.

Sports and Recreation

What sports are popular in this country? Include team sports as well as individual sports.

List any winners of the Olympic Gold Medal since 1972. Name the sport the medal was received for.

What games do children play with their friends? Which of these games are new to you?

How do the land features and climate of this country affect the most popular sports and games?

Ready to Report ©THE MONKEY SISTERS, INC.

Map of _____

Draw a map of the country. Label and indicate the capital city with a star. Show three other major cities, principal rivers and lakes and the major mountain ranges. Indicate the countries that border this country. This map will be submitted with your written report.

Name _____

STUDENT PLANNING SHEET FOR REPORT ON FAMOUS LANDMARKS

Your assignment is to do research on a famous landmark and use the facts to write a report.

You may select from the following choices: The Eiffel Tower, The Parthenon, The Liberty Bell, The Empire State Building, Mount Rushmore, The Leaning Tower of Pisa, The Taj Mahal, The Lincoln Memorial, and The White House or you may choose another landmark approved by your teacher.

You may use some or all of the following resource materials in gathering your information:
- encyclopedias
- almanacs
- library books
- magazines
- filmstrips, videos or television shows about this landmark
- picture files and photographs
- travel brochures and tourist guides

For the first part of this assignment, you will _write notes_ in the frames on the following pages. This information does not need to be in complete sentences. Write only enough words to use later in writing your report.

The following guide will help you in organizing your work:
- Use _at least three_ sources to gather your facts. Keep a bibliography of all your sources—title, author, publisher, copyright date, issue, volume, etc.
- Look at pictures and photographs to learn about the different kinds of landmarks.
- Fill in the following pages with facts as you do your research.
- When these pages are complete, you will be ready to use the notes to write your report.
- Do not throw away your note pages. You will need to submit them along with your written report.

Writing your report:
- Use the facts on the _Introductory Information_ page to develop your opening paragraph.
- Plan the rest of your report—writing one paragraph for each page of notes—in the following order:
    —building the landmark
    —structure and design
    —visiting the landmark
    —of special interest
    —pictures and photographs
- Your last paragraph should be a conclusion and interesting summary.
- List your sources on a separate sheet titled 'Bibliography.' This page will follow your pictures and photographs.
- Reread your report. Make any changes and correct any errors.
- Rewrite your report using a neat, legible handwriting.
- The report should be complete and ready to submit by _____
- Design an appealing cover and give your report an interesting title.

Ready to Report ©THE MONKEY SISTERS, INC.

INTRODUCTORY INFORMATION

What landmark have you chosen for your report? Why did you select it?

Where is this landmark located?

Why do you think this location was selected?

What makes this landmark famous?

Ready to Report © THE MONKEY SISTERS, INC.

BUILDING THE LANDMARK

When was this structure built? How many years did it take to complete it? In what year was it completed?

How did the landmark get its name?

Is this landmark dedicated to someone special or was it built for a special architectural reason? Explain.

Did this structure ever suffer severe damage or destruction? If so, explain what happened and how it has been restored.

STRUCTURE AND DESIGN

Describe the design of this landmark.

Who was the architect/designer of this structure?

How is this landmark special in design?

What materials were used to build this structure?

What problems, if any, arose during its construction?

VISITING THE LANDMARK

Can you climb to the top of this landmark? If so, what would take you to the top—steps, an elevator, or both?

What would you see from the top?

What would be pointed out of special interest if you were on a guided tour?

Why do people come to see this landmark? Is there a charge for touring or viewing it? If so, what is the charge?

OF SPECIAL INTEREST

Name two historic or newsworthy events that took place at this landmark.

What famous people have been associated with it over the years? Explain.

Were any records achieved in building this landmark? Was it the first, highest, longest, etc.? Explain.

If any records were achieved, has this been surpassed at a later date? If so, name the newer structure and tell how the record was surpassed.

Ready to Report © THE MONKEY SISTERS, INC.

PICTURES AND PHOTOGRAPHS

Show at least three pictures or photographs of this landmark. You may attach any of the following:

- copies of photographs from books and magazines
- photographs cut from travel brochures
- picture post cards
- photographs of this landmark your family may have (these will be returned!)

You may attach a second sheet if necessary.

ANSWER KEY

WHALES

Page 2:

A whale is a large, warm-blooded, lung-breathing mammal. Its tail has two flukes. Their skeletal, vascular, digestive, respiratory, sensory and reproductive features are similiar to other mammals rather than fish in spite of their general resemblance to fish.

Baleen whales and toothed whales. The adult baleen whale has no teeth. Toothed whales have many teeth in their lower jaw. Toothed whales produce ambergris. Baleen whales have two blowholes; toothed whales have one.

Whales are mammals: they are lung-breathing, warm-blooded and give birth to live young offspring and feed them with milk.

Dolphins and porpoises are toothed whales. They have teeth and one blowhole.

Page 3:

Blubber: a white, rubbery layer of fat in whales that helps retain body heat in water that is always colder than their body temperature.

Blowhole: a hole for the escape of air; a nostril in the top of the head of a whale.

Fluke: a lobe of the whale's tail.

Baleen: also known as whalebone; it is a horny substance attached in two rows along the upper jaw—the material is similar to human fingernails.

Ambergris: a waxy substance formed in the intestine or stomach of the sperm whale. It is a valuable substance used in the manufacture of perfume.

Page 4:

A whale has the same basic shape as a fish. In many whales, the head makes up one-third of the body length. It has two flippers to help steer and keep its balance. The tail has two flukes—the tail fins are sideways, not up and down like fish. The skin is not covered with hair like other mammals. It is smooth and rubbery.

Page 5:

The largest whale is the blue whale. It can be up to 100 feet long.

An average adult whale can be anywhere from 4 feet to 100 feet and weigh from (1.2 to 30.5 meters) 100 lbs. to 150 tons. (45.4 kilograms to 136.077 metric tons).

It takes two years to reach adult size.

Dolphins and porpoises are small whales. A dolphin can be from 7 to 30 feet (2.1 to 9 meters). A porpoise can be from 4 to 6 feet (1.2 to 1.8 meters).

Page 6:

The baleen whale has no teeth but plates of baleen suspended from the upper jaw. The baleen are used for straining out small fish from sand that is scooped up. They have two blowholes.

Three groups of baleen whales are: right whales, gray whales and rorquals.

Page 7:

The main difference from baleen whales is that toothed whales have teeth.

Five groups of toothed whales are: sperm whales, beaked whales, belugas and narwhals, dolphins and porpoises, and river whales.

Page 8:

Baleen whales feed on plankton, krill, herring, and sardines.

Large toothed whales feed on large squid and fish. Killer whales eat marine mammals (dolpins, porpoises and seals) as well as penguins, salmon and shark. Dolphins and porpoises feed on fish.

They leave the waters of the Arctic when the water freezes over. In the winter they go to the warmer subtropical waters where pairing takes place and the young are born. Warm waters are excellent environments for babies who don't have a layer of blubber to keep them warm. The California gray whale migrates along the west coast of the United States and the humpback migrates to the coast of New Zealand.

The Arctic area is rich in plankton. Whales spend their time prior to winter feeding and storing reserves of blubber.

ALASKA

Page 11:

Alaska is an adaptation of the Eskimo word, Alakshak meaning mainland. Another belief is that the word means 'the great country.'

591,004 sq. miles (1,530,693 sq. km.). It is approximately one-fifth the size of the continental United States.

The state capital is Juneau. The largest city is Anchorage. The highest point is Mt. McKinley in Denali National Park. It is 20,320 feet or 6,194 meters.

The flag is a field of dark blue with seven gold stars in the lower left representing the Big Dipper and one gold star in the upper right representing Polaris.

Page 12:

The four major land regions are the Pacific Mountain System, Central Uplands and Lowlands, Rocky Mountain System and the Arctic Coastal System.

Principal rivers are the Yukon and Kuskokwim.

Matanuska Valley of the Pacific Mountain System is the most productive farmland.

The Alaska Peninsula and Aleutian Islands are in the southwest. There are 14 large islands and 55 small islands.

Page 13:

The greatest rainfall is along the southeast coast. In Juneau, the annual rainfall is about 90 inches (228.6 m).

The largest glaciers are between Glacier Bay and Prince William Sound and the Alaska/Canada boundary of southeastern Alaska.

The mildest climate is in southern Alaska.

Average temperatures in January: -9 degrees F (-23 degrees C).
Average temperatues in July: 59 degrees F (15 degrees C).

Page 14:

Fish: Fishing and marketing of salmon, king crab, halibut, herring and shrimp has been very important to Alaska's economy. Fishing is a top source of employment.

Sea Mammals: Whales provide food for Eskimos and fats to whalers. The fur seal has been used for its fur.

Big Game Animals: Hunting of moose, elk, caribou and deer.

Fur-bearing Animals: These animals are hunted for their fur: fox, sable, ermine, mink, beaver, muskrat.

Page 15:

Four leading industries are fisheries, paper products, lumber and wood pulp production, and mining (petroleum, natural gas, sand and gravel, stone, gold).

Abundant fuels are petroleum, natural gas and coal.

Three main sources of work are construction companies, fisheries, mining and lumber/paper manufacturing.

Page 16:

Cabbage, lettuce, cauliflower, potatoes, beets, and carrots grow well and extra large due to 20 hours of sun. The crops ripen quickly. The rigorous winters limit crops to hardy root vegetables and grains. The growing season is 60-100 days.

The dairy industry is most productive in southern Alaska near Anchorage.

Blueberries, raspberries and strawberries grow well.

Wheat, oats, rye and barley grow well in the interior region.

Page 17:

The Eskimo's skin is light yellowish-brown, their hair is straight and black and their faces are broad with high cheekbones. Their noses are generally flat; eyes are black.

Eskimos mainly live along the coast of the Arctic, the Bering Sea and the Gulf of Alaska.

Eskimos are adept at ivory carving, basketry, jade carving and wood carving.

Eskimos are employed in commercial fisheries, petroleum mining and prospecting, and construction.

Ready to Report © THE MONKEY SISTERS, INC.

Page 18:

Boundaries: north-Arctic Ocean; east-Canada (Yukon Territory and British Columbia); south-Pacific Ocean and Gulf of Alaska; west-Bering Sea and Bering Strait.

THE STATUE OF LIBERTY

Page 20:

It is located on Liberty Island in New York Harbor or upper New York Bay in New York City.

The original name was Bedloe's Island. It was changed in 1956.

The statue was dedicated on October 28, 1886.

Immigrants who came to the U.S. during this time arrived by ship only. They had to stop at Ellis Island for processing and health exams before entering the U.S. and had to pass the Statue of Liberty on their way to Ellis Island.

Page 21:

It was built in Paris, France and took 11 years to build (1875-1886).

The arm holding the torch and head was built first. This was sent to Philadelphia, PA for America's 100th birthday celebration in 1876. Afterward, it stood in Madison Square in New York City for several years. Liberty's head was shown at the World's Fair in Paris during this time. Visitors were able to climb around and look inside. In this way, money was raised to pay for the statue.

France paid for building the statue. Money was raised by people looking inside the head at the World's Fair.

The U.S. paid for the pedestal. Joseph Pulitzer, a New York newspaper publisher, helped with the fund-raising. People all over the country, as well as school children, sent in donations. Mr. Pulitzer printed the names of all people who donated money.

Problems were created by dismantling, crating and shipping the statue across the Atlantic. Also, the pedestal was not completed when the statue was.

Page 22:

Frederic Auguste Bartholdi of France was the sculptor.

Alexandre Gustave Eiffel constructed the skeleton. He is the man who built the Eiffel Tower.

Richard Morris Hunt designed the pedestal.

The statue was taken completely apart. Each piece was marked and packed into a crate. There were 214 crates in all. They were carried by train and then put on a ship to the U.S.

Page 23:

The torch is a symbol of welcome to voyagers coming to the U.S.

July 4, 1776—this is the date the Declaration of Independence was signed.

The 7 spikes represent the 7 seas and 7 continents.

The broken chain and foot thrust forwards indicates progress from bondage to freedom.

Page 24:

The poet was Emma Lazarus.

"Give me your tired, your poor,
Your huddled masses yearning to breathe free,
The wretched refuse of your teeming shore,
Send these, the homeless, tempest-tost to me,
I lift my lamp beside the golden door!"

Answers will vary in reasons for inscription.

Page 25:

Restoration began in 1983.

The goal was to restore the Statue and then Ellis Island and to establish a fund for future repairs. Donations from businesses and individuals from the U.S. as well as France helped raise money.

Restoration included a new stairway in the statue; the torch was removed and rebuilt; the internal structural supports were replaced; new viewing platforms were installed at the top of the pedestal; the copper skin was cleaned; the viewing platform at the crown was rebuilt; a new all-glass elevator was installed in the pedestal.

At the completion of the restoration, the 100th birthday of the Statue of Liberty was celebrated on July 4, 1986.

Page 26:

Copper, when new, is a brown metallic color. When it is exposed to air, it oxidizes, and if it is not polished, will turn green.

It is a museum of immigration designed to show how millions of people from almost every country came to the U.S. and built a great nation. Displays show how the Indians came to America; how European immigrants made the journey by ship; and the ethnic groups that make up the American people. There are maps, paintings, films, dioramas and taped interviews with more than 100 immigrants.

The National Park Service oversees the care and maintenance of the Statue. They were responsible for working with the Statue of Liberty-Ellis Island Centennial Commission and the French-American Committee for restoration. The National Park Service is responsible for the daily maintenance as well as future repairs.

Page 27:

Foundation to torch:	151'1	(46.05m)
Base to torch:	305'1"	(92.99m)
Torch:	21"	(6.4m)
Across an eye:	2'6"	(76cm)
Length of nose:	4'6"	(1.37cm)
Width of mouth:	3'	(91cm)
Length of right arm:	42'	(12.80m)
Size of fingernail:	13"x10"	(33cm x 25cm)
Tablet:	23'7" x 13'7"	(7.19m x 4.14m)
Total weight:	225 tons	
Steps from base to crown:	171	
Steps in pedestal:	167	
Windows in crown:	25	
Spikes in crown:	7	

(Metric conversions are approximate)

The Copper Lady, Liberty Enlightening the World, Miss Liberty, Lady Liberty, Lady with the Lamp, Mother of Exiles.

PRINCE CHARLES

Page 29:

A monarchy is a country ruled by a monarch; a title only achieved by birth, not by election.

As the first-born son of Queen Elizabeth, Prince Charles will become King Charles when she dies or abdicates the throne.

The rulers are a king or queen. The queen can be a monarch only by birth, not by being the wife of a king.

The current monarch is Queen Elizabeth.

Prince of Wales is the title borne by the eldest son or heir apparent of the British sovereign.

Page 30:

Royalty is royal station achieved by birth.

Parents: Queen Elizabeth and Prince Philip, Duke of Edinburgh
Sisters and brothers: Prince Andrew, Prince Edward, Princess Anne
Wife and Children: Diana, Princess of Wales; (wife)
                     Prince Harry and Prince William (children)—
                     as of 1988

Prince Harry would be next in line. He is the eldest son of the heir apparent, Prince Charles. Prince Charles' sons take precedence over Prince Charles' brothers.

Page 31:

He lived in a 600-room palace, had a private detective, a chauffeur, nannies and servants.

He was taught by a governess in the palace.

Math was most difficult.

He was interested in horseback riding and swimming.

Ready to Report ©THE MONKEY SISTERS, INC.

Page 32:

He started attending a regular class at age 8.

The first school was Hill House, a boy's school for children of diplomats and government families.

Some problems were the presence of newspaper reporters and cameramen who hung around the school trying to photograph Prince Charles.

He had private lessons in the morning with his governess/teacher at the palace. In the afternoon, he attended classes where he could participate in games and physical activities with other children.

Page 33:

He attended Cheam School next. This is the oldest prep school in England. It was chosen because it offered a wide range of activities and training that would help prepare Prince Charles as future king.

He had difficulty making friends, he was poor in math, it was his first time away from home and the dormitory conditions were very meager in comparison to the palace.

Next, he attended Gordonstoun. This school is molded after a blend of German aristocratic tradition and the best of English education. Great emphasis is placed on service to others in the community and on physical activities and attainments. Students are encouraged to develop a sense of charity, inner strength, self-control and courage.

The goal of the school is to create a balance between the physical and the mental with emphasis on self-reliance that would help produce a well-rounded human being.

His best subjects were Latin, French, history, English language and literature.

Page 34:

He served in the Royal Air Force and Royal Navy and excelled as a helicopter pilot.

He was 33 years old when he married. The wedding took place on July 29, 1981. The wedding was viewed by all the world on television and it was described as a 'fairy-tale' wedding with the bride arriving at the church in a covered carriage.

His main duties include being available for special ceremonies, visiting hospitals and institutions for the underprivileged, and taking part in official duties as part of the royal family.

Highgrove House is his official residence. He lives at Kensington Palace in London much of the time. He also vacations with his family at Sandringham, Balmoral and Windsor Castle.

He enjoys polo, hunting, shooting, horseback riding and fishing. He prefers sports that require individual skill rather than team games.

OLYMPICS

Page 36:

The ancient Olympics were first held in 776 B.C. The event was the 200 meter run.

The event was held in the Valley of Olympia, Greece.

The ancient Olympics had one winner.

The prize was a crown of olive branches and leaves.

The ancient Olympics ended in 394 A.D. They had been held for nearly 1200 years.

Page 37:

Pierre de Coubertin, from France was credited with starting the new series of Olympics.

The first modern Olympics were held in the summer of 1896 in Athens, Greece.

The International Olympic Committee organizes the games, makes the rules and selects the cities.

Amateur means that an athlete has never earned money from sports.

Olympic games would be held every four years in a different city.

Page 38:

The athletes from Greece enter first to remind people that the Olympics began in Greece.

The rings are black, blue, green, red and yellow representing Africa, Asia, Australia, Europe, North and South America.

Relays of runners carry the torch. The flame may be sent by boat or airplane or laser beam if oceans must be crossed.

The final runner brings the torch into the stadium and lights the Olympic flame which burns throughout the games.

At the end of the opening ceremonies, doves are released as a symbol of peace.

Page 39:

Three medals are given for each final event.

First place is the gold medal; second place is the silver medal; third place is the bronze medal.

When the winners receive their medals, the flags of the winners countries are raised and a band plays the national anthem of the gold medal winner's country.

Teams and individuals can win prizes. Countries cannot win.

Page 40:

The following athletes are among those listed as Olympic champions:

Paavo Nurmi, Finnish runner, 9 medals 1920-1928
Larisa Latynina, Russian gymnast, 9 medals, 1956-1964
Mark Spitz, American swimmer, 9 medals, 1968-1972
Johnny Weissmuller, American swimmer, 5 medals, 1924-1928
Sonja Henie, Norwegian figure skater, 3 medals, 1928-1936
Eric Heiden, American speed-skater, 5 medals, 1980
Nadia Comaneci, Romanian gymnast, 3 medals, 1976
Wilma Rudolph, American runner, 3 medals, 1960
Jesse Owens, American track and field, 4 medals, 1936.

Page 41:

To be an Olympic athlete, the athlete must be an amateur. The athlete must make the team for his country. Each country has an Olympic Committee and holds selection trials. The best athletes make the team. To get invited to the selection trials, an athlete must have done well in amateur or college sports.

Athletes compete to bring honor to their country and to prove they are the best in the world.

Approximately 151 countries participate. There are 22 sports. New sports are added from time to time.

Winter sports: bobsled (men only); figure skating, ice hockey (men only); luge, skiing, speed skating.

Summer sports: track and field, water sports, basketball, field hockey, soccer, team handball, volleyball, tennis, table tennis, gymnastics, boxing, wrestling, judo, fencing, weight-lifting, archery, shooting, equestrian sports, cycling.

Page 42:

Separate events are held for men and women because it is not fair to compete against each other in most sports. There are different rules and different equipment for men and women.

25 countries must play the sport for it to be in the Olympics.

At least 12 countries must enter the Olympic competition.

Women began to participate in 1900 in Paris.

In 1924 the games were divided into two parts—winter and summer games. Winter games are held in January or February before the summer games.

Olympic Games were not held in 1940 and 1944 because of World War II.

Page 43:

Answers will vary.